MY GRATITUDE JOURNAL

My Gratitude Journal

BY
DR. CHRISTINE TOPJIAN

Authors Get Published www.authorsgetpublished.com

CONTENTS

DEDICATIONS - ix
HOW YOU CAN USE YOUR BOOK - xi

January 1
1

Scripture

February 1
34

Quote

March 1
66

Scripture

April 1
98

Quote

May 1

130

Quote

June 1

162

Scripture

July 1

194

Quote

August 1

226

Quote

September 1

258

Quote

October 1

290

Quote

November 1
322

Quote

December 1
354

Scripture

EXTRA PAGES - 387

Copyright © 2023 by By Dr. Christine Topjian

All rights reserved. No part of this book may be reproduced in any manner whatsoever without written permission except in the case of brief quotations embodied in critical articles and reviews.

First Printing, 2023

Published By Authors Get Published
An Imprint of Christine Topjian Publishing
Toronto, ON

www.AuthorsGetPublished.com

DEDICATIONS

This gratitude book is dedicated to each person who has goals, wishes and dreams that they wish to fulfill and who chooses to give thanks for what they already have, thereby inviting more goodness into their lives.

I hope that this book helps bring to light all the goodness you have already received from God and serves as a daily reminder of that.

HOW YOU CAN USE YOUR BOOK

Because gratitude can be given at any time, I wanted to make this a book you can start at any time and that will last you the entire year. Whether you start jotting down your gratitude at the beginning of a new month or any other time, the act of doing this is very powerful and as magnets, you are attracting more good into your life. This is how God set things up for us.

I also hope that you will find the encouraging quote or Scripture at the end of each month to be very helpful.

Each time you complete a time of gratitude (whether at the end of the day, at the end of the week, or however you decide to do this) reward yourself and remind yourself that you are really doing a great job by engaging in this and by dedicating time to doing this.

JANUARY 1

JANUARY 2

JANUARY 3

JANUARY 4

JANUARY 5

JANUARY 6

JANUARY 7

JANUARY 8

JANUARY 9

JANUARY 10

JANUARY 11

JANUARY 12

JANUARY 13

JANUARY 14

JANUARY 15

JANUARY 16

JANUARY 17

JANUARY 18

JANUARY 19

JANUARY 20

JANUARY 21

JANUARY 22

JANUARY 23

JANUARY 24

JANUARY 25

JANUARY 26

JANUARY 27

JANUARY 28

JANUARY 29

JANUARY 30

JANUARY 31

Scripture

Matthew 7:7

"Ask and it will be given to you; seek and you will find; knock and the door will be opened to you."

FEBRUARY 1

FEBRUARY 2

FEBRUARY 3

FEBRUARY 4

FEBRUARY 5

FEBRUARY 6

FEBRUARY 7

FEBRUARY 8

FEBRUARY 9

FEBRUARY 10

FEBRUARY 11

FEBRUARY 12

FEBRUARY 13

FEBRUARY 14

FEBRUARY 15

FEBRUARY 16

FEBRUARY 17

FEBRUARY 18

FEBRUARY 19

FEBRUARY 20

FEBRUARY 21

FEBRUARY 22

FEBRUARY 23

FEBRUARY 24

FEBRUARY 25

FEBRUARY 26

FEBRUARY 27

FEBRUARY 28

FEBRUARY 29

FEBRUARY 30

Quote

Be the change you want to see in the world.

- Mahatma Gandhi

MARCH 1

MARCH 2

MARCH 3

MARCH 4

MARCH 5

MARCH 6

MARCH 7

MARCH 8

MARCH 9

MARCH 10

MARCH 11

MARCH 12

MARCH 13

MARCH 14

MARCH 15

MARCH 16

MARCH 17

MARCH 18

MARCH 19

MARCH 20

MARCH 21

MARCH 22

MARCH 23

MARCH 24

MARCH 25

MARCH 26

MARCH 27

MARCH 28

MARCH 29

MARCH 30

MARCH 31

Scripture

1 Thessalonian 5:16-18

"Rejoice always, pray continually, give thanks in all circumstances; for this is God's will for you in Christ Jesus."

APRIL 1

APRIL 2

APRIL 3

APRIL 4

APRIL 5

APRIL 6

APRIL 7

APRIL 8

APRIL 9

APRIL 10

APRIL 11

APRIL 12

APRIL 13

APRIL 14

APRIL 15

APRIL 16

APRIL 17

APRIL 18

APRIL 19

APRIL 20

APRIL 21

APRIL 22

APRIL 23

APRIL 24

APRIL 25

APRIL 26

APRIL 27

APRIL 28

APRIL 29

APRIL 30

Quote

"Be grateful for all that you have, because someone out there is wishing for what you already have."

Dr. Christine Topjian

MAY 1

MAY 2

MAY 3

MAY 4

MAY 5

MAY 6

MAY 7

MAY 8

MAY 9

MAY 10

MAY 11

MAY 12

MAY 13

MAY 14

MAY 15

MAY 16

MAY 17

MAY 18

MAY 19

MAY 20

MAY 21

MAY 22

MAY 23

MAY 24

MAY 25

MAY 26

MAY 27

MAY 28

MAY 29

MAY 30

MAY 31

Quote

"One of the secrets of a happy life is continuous small treats."

— *Iris Murdoch*

JUNE 1

JUNE 2

JUNE 3

JUNE 4

JUNE 5

JUNE 6

JUNE 7

JUNE 8

JUNE 9

JUNE 10

JUNE 11

JUNE 12

JUNE 13

JUNE 14

JUNE 15

JUNE 16

JUNE 17

JUNE 18

JUNE 19

JUNE 20

JUNE 21

JUNE 22

JUNE 23

JUNE 24

JUNE 25

JUNE 26

JUNE 27

JUNE 28

JUNE 29

JUNE 30

Scripture

Colossians 3:23

Whatever you do, work at it with all your heart, as working for the Lord, not for human masters.

JULY 1

JULY 2

JULY 3

JULY 4

JULY 5

JULY 6

JULY 7

JULY 8

JULY 9

JULY 10

JULY 11

JULY 12

JULY 13

JULY 14

JULY 15

JULY 17

JULY 18

JULY 19

JULY 20

JULY 21

JULY 22

JULY 23

JULY 24

JULY 25

JULY 26

JULY 27

JULY 28

JULY 29

JULY 30

JULY 31

Quote

"Gratitude turns what we have into enough."

– Anonymous.

AUGUST 1

AUGUST 2

AUGUST 3

AUGUST 4

AUGUST 5

AUGUST 6

AUGUST 7

AUGUST 8

AUGUST 9

AUGUST 10

AUGUST 11

AUGUST 12

AUGUST 13

AUGUST 14

AUGUST 15

AUGUST 16

AUGUST 17

AUGUST 18

AUGUST 19

AUGUST 20

AUGUST 21

AUGUST 22

AUGUST 23

AUGUST 24

AUGUST 25

AUGUST 26

AUGUST 27

AUGUST 28

AUGUST 29

AUGUST 30

AUGUST 31

Quote

"Everything we do should be a result of our gratitude for what God has done for us."

- Lauryn Hill

SEPTEMBER 1

SEPTEMBER 2

SEPTEMBER 3

SEPTEMBER 4

SEPTEMBER 5

SEPTEMBER 6

SEPTEMBER 7

SEPTEMBER 8

SEPTEMBER 9

SEPTEMBER 10

SEPTEMBER 11

SEPTEMBER 12

SEPTEMBER 13

SEPTEMBER 14

SEPTEMBER 15

SEPTEMBER 16

SEPTEMBER 17

SEPTEMBER 18

SEPTEMBER 19

SEPTEMBER 20

SEPTEMBER 21

SEPTEMBER 22

SEPTEMBER 23

SEPTEMBER 24

SEPTEMBER 25

SEPTEMBER 26

SEPTEMBER 27

SEPTEMBER 28

SEPTEMBER 29

SEPTEMBER 30

Quote

"This is a wonderful day. I have never seen this one before."

- Maya Angelou

OCTOBER 1

OCTOBER 2

OCTOBER 3

OCTOBER 4

OCTOBER 6

OCTOBER 7

OCTOBER 8

OCTOBER 9

OCTOBER 10

OCTOBER 11

OCTOBER 12

OCTOBER 13

OCTOBER 14

OCTOBER 15

OCTOBER 16

OCTOBER 17

OCTOBER 18

OCTOBER 19

OCTOBER 20

OCTOBER 21

OCTOBER 22

OCTOBER 23

OCTOBER 24

OCTOBER 25

OCTOBER 26

OCTOBER 27

OCTOBER 28

OCTOBER 29

OCTOBER 30

OCTOBER 31

Quote

"Appreciation is a wonderful thing. It makes what is excellent in others belong to us as well."

- Voltaire

NOVEMBER 1

NOVEMBER 2

NOVEMBER 2

NOVEMBER 3

NOVEMBER 4

NOVEMBER 5

NOVEMBER 6

NOVEMBER 7

NOVEMBER 8

NOVEMBER 9

NOVEMBER 10

NOVEMBER 11

NOVEMBER 12

NOVEMBER 13

NOVEMBER 14

NOVEMBER 15

NOVEMBER 16

NOVEMBER 17

NOVEMBER 18

NOVEMBER 19

NOVEMBER 20

NOVEMBER 21

NOVEMBER 22

NOVEMBER 23

NOVEMBER 24

NOVEMBER 25

NOVEMBER 26

NOVEMBER 27

NOVEMBER 28

NOVEMBER 29

NOVEMBER 30

Quote

"When I started counting my blessings, my whole life turned around."

- Willie Nelson

DECEMBER 1

DECEMBER 2

DECEMBER 3

DECEMBER 4

DECEMBER 5

DECEMBER 6

DECEMBER 7

DECEMBER 8

DECEMBER 9

DECEMBER 10

DECEMBER 11

DECEMBER 12

DECEMBER 13

DECEMBER 14

DECEMBER 15

DECEMBER 16

DECEMBER 17

DECEMBER 19

DECEMBER 20

DECEMBER 21

DECEMBER 22

DECEMBER 23

DECEMBER 24

DECEMBER 25

DECEMBER 26

DECEMBER 27

DECEMBER 28

DECEMBER 29

DECEMBER 30

DECEMBER 31

Scripture

Phillipians 4:6

Do not be anxious about anything, but in everything by prayer and supplication with thanksgiving let your requests be made known to God.

EXTRA PAGES

These extra pages have been provided for your convenience. In the event that you wanted to jot down some notes, jot down some more gratitude or just had some musings that you want to keep track of, this space has been provided for those reasons.

Extra Pages

www.ingramcontent.com/pod-product-compliance
Lightning Source LLC
Chambersburg PA
CBHW060406010526
44107CB00005B/604